I0481987

Habits Of Highly Effective People

What Are The Habits Of Successful People?

LELA GIBSON

Copyright © 2017 Lela Gibson

All rights reserved.

CONTENTS

Introduction

I want to thank you and congratulate you for buying the book, *"Habits Of Highly Effective People"*.

This book contains proven steps and strategies on how to build habits to become effective.

Judging from your interest in the title of this book, it is right to assume that as an individual, you are someone interested in forming habits that help you achieve great success in whatever undertaking: financial success, weight loss success, relationship success, productivity, etc. This assumption draws upon the notion that to achieve immense success in your life, you have to be, undoubtedly, effective.

Unfortunately, if you are like most people, which rightly, you are, unless you have a strand of super alien DNA that allows you to ninja your way through habit formation, in which case, you should patent yourself and sell you DNA to the masses, you are amongst the many who struggle with the process of creating lasting habits. Like most, even though you start practicing things/habits that promise to bring you success, after practicing these things for a few days, your desire to practice them reduces and you resort to bad habits that deny you success.

Even more unfortunate is the fact that most books on the habit change subject rally on and on about how, to live an effective, and as such, a successful life, you should adopt so and so habit, but rarely do they guide you through the process of habit change or show you how to make these 'success' habits sticky.

If there is one thing we know about habits, it is this: *adopting a habit is, at first, easy;* however, turning something you do one day into something you do every day, the very definition of a habit, is not easy.

In this regard, this book is different because:

1. It starts by outlining why habits are at the core of success and why adopting the right habits will determine how effective and successful you are in life.

2. It takes you by the hand and guides you through the process of habit change; it teaches you how to get started on doing something one day and keep doing it until it turns into a habit.

3. This habits guide shows you, in a step-by-step manner, how to adopt specific habits that will lead you to success in everything you do.

If you are ready to change your life for good, get started with this guide TODAY! You will be thankful you did.

Thanks again for buying this book. I hope you enjoy it!

The Power Of Habits: How Habits Influence Success

Ponder over these questions:

What do you habitually think of first when you wake up? What do you do first thing in the morning as you get out of bed when you are still shaking off the cobwebs of that sweet, morning sleep? Do you dreamily make your way to the toilet, or before sitting down on the toilet seat, do you reach for your toothbrush and brush your teeth as you do your business? What do you do?

Pay special attention to your answers to these questions because as you will come to notice, habits are essentially things you do without much thought or consideration.

Defining Habits

In his book, *The Story of Philosophy: The Lives and Opinions of the World's Greatest Philosophers*, Will Durant, one of America's greatest writers, historians, and philosophers best known for, in collaboration with his wife, creating 11 volumes of the story of civilization, a groundbreaking piece of work that helped popularize philosophy, said:

"We are what we repeatedly do. Excellence, then, is not an act, but a habit."

This is the best description of habits: habits are things we repeatedly do. In retrospect, Will's quote is also the best show of how habits influence our every day life.

If you plop down onto your couch each evening after work, and you do this every day, this is your habit. If when your alarm beeps to signal your wake up time, instead of getting out of bed, you hit the snooze button, and you do this day in day out, this is a habit. At the core of habits is automation: *when something becomes a habit, you no longer use conscious effort to engage in it: you simply do.*

Going back to the questions in the first part of this section, what do you do first thing in the morning? If you wake up and make your way to the loo, do you use any mental effort? The answer is no; the reason behind this is because you have made your way to the loo in the morning so many times that your brain has created an automatic program for this behavior. The same applies to an idea such as exercising or meditating at a specific time of day every day.

Now that we have defined habits—*habits are things we do so repeatedly that they become automatic*—let us consider how habits affect our lives.

How Habits Influence Our Lives And Success

As you may have derived from our previous discussion, because habits are things we do repeatedly, naturally, we have good and bad habits that have various effects on our lives.

To expound on, and illustrate this, let us go back and use our earlier example where immediately after getting home from work, you plop down into the comforting embrace of your couch, and remote in hand, proceed to watch hours of your favorite TV show. 2 or 3 hours later, you reach for the phone, order take-out, sink back into your couch, and proceed to gobble down the pizza or whatever take-out you fancy as you watch TV into the wee hours of the morning. You do this every day.

In this scenario, what do you think most likely: you have a lean, fit body and your life is a success-laden story, or you epitomize the modern day American who wages a constant battle with excess weight, lack of success or progress, and struggles with effectiveness or time management: which do you think most probable? The latter is likely to be your case because of one simple thing: *you have bad habits.*

On the other hand, consider a scenario where after getting home from work, instead of gluing your butt to your super comfortable couch, you head straight into your bedroom, take off the day's clothes, get into your gym clothes, and proceed to engage in any form of exercise.

After this, you shower, plan and compartmentalize your work for the following day. You then read an inspirational book or the bible, follow this up with something that increases your value as a valued member of your workplace or society in general, and after, proceed to make (or order) a healthy meal.

In this scenario, what do you think most probable: that you have a healthy mind and body and successful in every area of your life, or that you are overweight and struggling to achieve semblances of success? The former is likely to be true. That is how habits affect your life.

When you adopt good positive habits that propel you towards the success you desire, habits such as exercising, reading, or personal development, you become highly successful in every area of your life. These hypotheticals vividly paint a picture of how habits influence our lives.

If your life is a series of bad habits (remember: habits define who we are), habits such as procrastination, lack of exercise, negative thinking (yes, negative thinking is habitual), consuming junk, and failing to plan, among others, you are likely to struggle with achieving any sort of success in your life.

On the other hand, if your life is a series of good habits, good habits such as the ones we described above such as meditation, self-improvement, exercise, healthy eating, etc.– you can bet success will come to you as easily as breathing: effortlessly.

To achieve success, therefore, you have to practice success habits, not just for one day, but repeatedly until that thing (activity) becomes habitual and automatic. Unfortunately, while this process seems such an easy one, at least on paper, the process of habit adoption or change is never an easy one.

To help you understand how to create new habits, break bad old habits, and replace them with new positive ones that drive you towards the success you crave, let us discuss the process of habit formation.

Habit Formation: How Habits Work

Let us go back to something we looked at earlier. *"We are what we repeatedly do..."* What does this imply? Mr. Durant's statement implies that what we do on a day-to-day basis is in essence, the very building blocks of our lives.

If we are highly effective at our work, automatically, we are effective in other areas of our lives and thus highly successful because effectiveness and success are correlated. On the other hand, if we procrastinate, put off tasks, and favor immediate gratification over long-term gratification, we are bound to experience lags in our productivity, effectiveness, and ultimately, success.

Even though this is common knowledge, very few know that everything habitual, whether that be exercising every day so we can have a lean body indicative of good health, saving some money to a financial independence savings plan, or even something as mundane as waking up early every morning, these things have something in common: they follow the same script. *Every habit you have and practice, whether good or bad, follows the same script.*

In his book, **The Power of Habits:** *Why We Do What We Do in Life and Business,* Charles Duhigg, a Pulitzer Prize winning reporter, journalist, and New York Times Bestselling author of several books, describes the process of habit formation or change in three steps, what we call the 3Rs of habit change.

The Habit Loop: The Habit Formation Framework

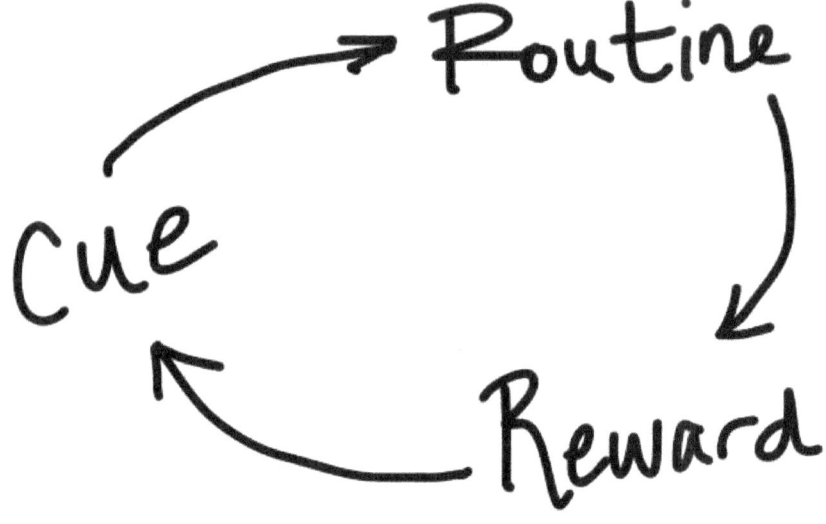

In this bestselling book, Mr. Duhigg postulates that every habit, good or bad, follows a 3-step pattern namely: **Reminder**, **Routine**, and **Reward**: the 3Rs (in the book, he calls it the habit loop and gives each of the three steps the following names: **cue**, **routine**, and **reward**

To help you understand how you habitually practice something (remember that at this point, we are talking about good and bad habits), let us break apart the three step process so we can deeply understand it because this understanding shall prove very helpful when we get started on the actual process of creating success habits that stick.

Let us start with the reminder or as Mr. Duhigg calls it, the cue.

Step 1: The Cue/Reminder

Consider the following. To wake up early, you set a 5 o'clock alarm. Once your alarm goes off, you either get up and prepare for your day, or you snooze the alarm several times and only wake up an hour or two later.

In this instance, as is clear for all to see, the 5 o'clock alarm is the cue/reminder that tells you "hey, it's time to wake up." As you know, reminders, such as those you set up on your phone to remind you to do something at a specific time or at a specific place, are anything that reminds you to do something.

In the process of habit formation, the cue or reminder can be anything. It can be walking into your door after a tiring day at work. It can be someone, a specific time, a location, emotional state, preceding action or anything.

To understand your habit, whichever habit, the first thing you need to do is understand the cue. To do that, you should ask yourself the following question: *"what triggers my X habit?"* For instance, *"What triggers my urge to procrastinate/etc.?"*

By asking yourself this question, you may discover that you procrastinate when work gets a bit tiresome. In any case, the cue is the thing/time/location/etc. that triggers a certain behavior.

Step 2: The Routine

The routine is relatively simple and straightforward to understand: once the cue appears or occurs, the routine is the behavior you engage in. In the example of the 5 o'clock alarm, waking up or snoozing the alarm once it chimes is the routine. In the case of the urge to put off work, once the cue appears, procrastination is the routine behavior you engage in.

To change a habit, you have to change the routine. Shortly, we shall discuss how to do that.

Step 3: The Reward

The reward is the benefit you gain from doing the routine. In the example of the routine of smoking, the nicotine high or the camaraderie of smoking in a group could be your reward. The reward is what motivates you to engage in a specific behavior.

Having looked at the process of habit formation, let us now look at how to create habits that stick. We shall make implementing this process as easy as possible.

How To Create Habits That Stick

To create habits that stick, you have to diagnose each individual habit you want to build, break, or replace, determine its loop, and then make changes to how you react once the cue presents itself.

NOTE: It is important to point out that in our case, the idea is to use the process described here to make habitual the success habits we shall discuss a bit later. Using the habit formation framework, we shall outline a systematic process you can use to create any lasting habit you want, assuming you want to cultivate good, success driven habits.

To create habits that stick, do the following:

1: Attach a Reminder to the New Habit

Assume the new habit you want to create is that of waking up early.

NOTE: Successful, effective, and productive people are early risers. You can navigate here to read about why successful people wake up early, and how waking up early influences your success and mindset.

To create this new habit, you have to create a reminder for the habit. In this instance, you could set an alarm for the time you want to wake up.

PS: Do you want to know the best time to wake up? Head here to see what scientific research has to say about the best time to wake up.

In the off chance that you have an alarm, instead of waking up once it goes off, you snooze, and go back to sleep, you do not need to change anything at this point. In such an instance, you only need to change the routine and the reward. We shall look at how to do that in the next steps.

When it comes to choosing a reminder, you are free to do what you please as long as the reminder you set helps you remember to engage in a specific routine or behavior. With that said however, to make the cue more effective, it is best to set up a visible cue (this of course depends on the habit you intend to create).

Another effective way to choose a good cue is to tie it to something you do each day. For instance, in the case of a 5 o'clock morning alarm, if you habitually reach for a glass of water placed at your bedside table at that time, you could set your morning alarm that as you reach for the water, the alarm dings and reminds you to wake up. The reasoning behind this is that it is easier to tie a reminder to something you habitually do.

Points To Note When Choosing Cues

Keep it very simple

When you choose harder to spot cues, you will realize that they hardly lend themselves to the automatic behaviors. Cues have to be simple, obvious and concrete- not abstract, complex, or vague.

Take a traffic light as an example; the red and green are usually opposite to each other (on the color wheel). The contrast is obvious and simple. The red light automatically cues braking. My point is that it would be harder to habitualize pressing the brakes at a light meant for 'go'.

"New"

It is also critical that you select a cue for a new behavior you are targeting that has limited pre-existing links with other behaviors. In other words, do not choose a cue that is already a cue for a number of other habits. The behavior you want to habitualize in this case might have to compete with other behaviors. If you cannot get a cue without strong links with other habits, the least you could do is pick a cue for a habit you need to replace.

2: Choose Your Habit

To complete the habit loop, you have to attach a routine to the cue. As described earlier, the routine is the behavior you engage in once the cue presents. In our instance, the cue is your morning alarm, and as such, the behavior is waking up.

This step applies to any habit you want to create. For instance, if you want to start exercising more in the morning, your cue to exercise could be seeing your gym clothes as you brush your teeth or as you make your way to the bathroom. Once you have the cue and the behavior, the other thing you have to do is tie the behavior to a reward.

Before we talk about experimenting with the reward:

NOTE: To break a bad habit, for instance snoozing your alarm each time it goes off, and instead of waking up, you pull the covers, you have to make the routine, which in this case, is leaving the warm embrace of your covers, easy to implement.

In such an instance, think of the simplest thing you need to do to get out of the warm covers. For instance, if you are a habitual alarm 'snoozer,' to snooze that alarm, you probably just stretch out your hand out of the covers in fear that the cold air of your bedroom will chip away at some of your glorious morning sleep.

If that is the case, find the easiest thing you can do to practice the routine that comes after the morning alarm cue; you could overcome the barrier by, once the alarm goes off, uncovering your whole body so you can experience the cool room temperature air of the morning. This air, because it is cooler than your body temperature as you are under the covers, shall sober you up. You can follow this up with hanging one foot over the bed and placing it onto the floor.

You can practice this tip with any habit you want to cultivate. For instance, if you set an exercise reminder, but each time the reminder says it is time to exercise, you procrastinate and find something else to do, determine the easiest way to start the exercise process.

If seeing your gym clothes as you brush your teeth is the cue for your exercise routine, the easiest thing to do would be to visualize yourself acing your exercise routine. This will motivate you to actually wear your gym clothes and head out for your morning exercise routine.

While we all want to adopt good habits as fast as possible, starting big is a sure way to fail. On the contrary, small changes are more manageable and easy to implement. This is why most habit change experts advise that to create a new habit or change an old one, you should start small, so small (and therefore easy) that you cannot say no.

For this reason, this effective habits guide advices you to determine the tinniest thing of the habit you want to adopt and then do that consistently. BJ Fogg, a leading human behavior change expert suggests that you should start so small that, "if the habit you want to create is that of flossing, you should start creating your habit by flossing one tooth."

To create habits that stick, in the very beginning, you should not worry about how well or how bad you are at that habit/behavior. Your only concern should be with making the behavior sticky. Creating habits that stick demands **consistency**. When you simplify things, consistency becomes super easy. On the other hand, if you overcomplicate a habit, sticking to it will become very difficult and you will give up.

If the new habit you want to create is that of waking up immediately after your alarm goes off, ask yourself this "what can I do to make this habit very easy to do?" You could start with the examples given earlier.

3: Experiment with the Reward

Rewards are the motivation behind every habit. You snooze that alarm because you want to enjoy the warmth of the covers and that glorious morning slumber. You smoke at a specific time or place because you want to enjoy the company of your smoking friends or nicotine high.

Everything we do in life (and in business) has some form of motivator; the reward is this motivator. To create habits that stick, you have to tie the new habits to a satisfying reward that completes the habit loop. To break old habits, you have to change the routine to one that gives you a reward similar to the one you experience whenever you practice the bad habit. This is where the need to experiment with different rewards comes in.

Rewards satisfy various cravings. Unfortunately, most of us are unconscious of the cravings driving most of our habits. As Mr. Duhigg states, most of our cravings are hiding in plain sight. To discover which cravings motivate certain behaviors/habits, you have to experiment with different rewards until you find a reward that compliments the behavior you want to adopt. In the case of behavior change, you have to experiment with various rewards until you find one that offers a reward similar to the one the habit you intend to break provides.

NOTE: This book shall not posit that to adopt a new habit or change a new one, you only need 21-days. As someone who has tried to adopt success habits or adopt habits that make you infinitely effective, you know that 21-days is not enough time to make a habit stick.

Rather than go with the common 21-days rule, this guide shall advice you to consider the habit you intend to adopt or change, and then give the habit formation process as much time as it needs. In this regard, it is important to remember that making some things habitual or breaking some bad habits that steal your productivity will take time.

In the first weeks or months of experimenting with rewards, simply consider yourself a curious scientist intent on collecting data. As stated earlier, do not concern yourself with how good or bad you are at practicing a certain behavior. Simply practice it and experiment with various rewards until you find one that works.

For instance, if your cue is the alarm, and the habit you want to break is that of sleeping past your wake up time, you could, on the first day, experiment with a midday snooze, see how that goes. On the next day, reward yourself with something you have been wanting to buy, do or get.

The idea here is to experiment with rewards until you find something that motivates you to practice something or in the case of breaking a habit that eats away at your productivity, experiment until you find a reward that satiates the craving that pushes you into practicing the bad habit.

As you experiment with rewards, note down how you feel after each cue, routine, reward loop. Note how you feel about the routine, the reward, and the things that come to mind as you do. Note down thoughts, reflections, emotions, feelings, etc. Writing forces you to be aware of the routine, the reward, and how they make you feel. It also allows you to be well aware of what you are thinking and feeling in that moment.

Once you determine which reward you are craving and the reward that shall satisfy that craving, consistently practice the routine, and offer yourself that reward until practicing the routine becomes automatic.

Always remember, *"Good habits, once established, are just as hard to break as are bad habits." -Robert Puller*

Highly Effective People Leave No Stones Unturned

As you have noted, creating good habits requires elimination of bad habits first, especially those that are in your way of creating good habits. What about an instance where you have bad habits that are not in any way affecting the good habits you want to create? For instance, what if you have adopted the habit of taking too much juice over your lunch break and you want to build a habit of talking to your employees nicely. These two don't not correlate, but when looked at from a broader perspective, both can have consequences to your success. They thus equally need your attention, especially if you are aiming for perfection.

Since we have discussed ways to replace bad habits with new ones, how can you eliminate the other bad habits, which we both know are hidden somewhere in your life (without necessarily looking to create a new habit)?

Here are some points on that:

Make the habit conscious

The first thing you have to do is find out when, and why you shout at your employees, drink too much juice over lunch break, or engage in any other undesirable habit. If you can notice the moment you are doing it, and the circumstances under which it is happening, and the feelings attached to it, you can find out why you are doing it and stop yourself dead in the tracks.

In fact, if you think about it, when stressed as you complete your bad habit, you essentially are not paying attention. When you pay attention, you are probably irritated: Irritated that you are feeling like this. Irritated that you are doing something you know is not right.

Pay attention; do not judge

When you are really watching what you are doing and observing how you are feeling, you can begin realizing that the bad habit is not helping solve the problem. You do not really feel better at all. This realization is critical; it is the key that will break the cycle.

I call this mindfulness; this is the sort of awareness mindfulness experts are always talking about: seeing clearly what is happening when you get lost in your behaviors and then becomes viscerally crestfallen. Over time, you learn to see the consequences of your actions; you are then empowered to let go of these habits.

It is, however, rather paradoxical that mindfulness is not entirely about having interest in, and getting close with what is happening in your body and mind; it is rather this willingness to turn to your experience as opposed to trying to make your bad cravings disappear as quickly as possible.

Remember, cravings disappear with time, but rarely do we pay attention to that part. When the internet connection in your home goes out, you feel frustrated at first, but then you find something else to do, you stop feeling frustrated.

Write it down so that it really sinks in

Janet L. Wolfe, PhD, a New York clinical psychologist and author of many bestselling books states that writing your bad habit down helps you establish a baseline.

"Write down the antecedents, all the emotions surrounding the yelling, and what goes through your mind when you shout at your employees." According to her, this will help make you more conscious of your undesirable habits. Here recommendation is that you keep the log for a minimum of one week, then after that, analyze the data and investigate your typical triggers. Do you engage in it when you are anxious or angry?

With such realizations, it is easier to find a solution.

Now that we have discussed how to create habits that stick, and how to break bad habits and replace them with new ones, let us discuss habits of the highly effective and successful; the habits you need to create and adopt to experience success in your life. Since the title of this book is "habits of the highly effective," the habits we shall discuss are those guaranteed to increase your productivity, and in extension, your success.

Habits Of The Effective And Successful

How effective you are at home and work determines how much success you achieve in life and the rate at which you achieve that success. To be successful, as successful as you can be in the shortest time possible, you have to, because as Mr. Durant said, we are what we repeatedly do, practice habits that make you as effective as possible and as such, as successful as possible.

This means you should replace bad habits such as procrastination with good habits such as the 5-minutes hack (the 5-minute hack is where you trick yourself into doing something for five minutes and continue doing so until you complete 50-60% of your work).

You should also replace bad habits such as binge watching TV with other good habits such as reading a book instead of watching some soap opera, or watching inspirational documentaries or interviews. The list of bad habits you can replace with good ones is endless.

The Habits You Need To Adopt To Achieve Success—With Practical Advice On How To Create Them

In this habits of the most successful and effective guide, we shall not concentrate on one specific habit. Instead, we shall discuss specific aspects of your personality that, after years and years of research, Steven R Covey, author of the internationally bestselling book **The 7 Habits of Highly Effective People**, illustrates that if you make them habitual, you shall be effective and successful in every venture you undertake.

Here is the first thing you need to work on:

1: Successful People Are Habitual Self-Masters

Mastery of the self is the most important habit you can cultivate. Leonardo Da Vinci rightfully said, *"One can have no smaller or greater mastery than mastery of oneself."* Never have there been truer words. If you can master yourself, you can conquer the world. In this case, what does self-mastery mean?

In its truest essence, self-mastery is the ability to make yourself do what is necessary even when you would rather not, or as Mr. Covey put it, mastery is, *"The ability to subordinate an impulse to a value is the essence of the proactive person."*

To illustrate this, we are going to use a simple habit: the habit of snoozing an alarm. Instead of following the cue that says you should wake up so you can enjoy the reward that comes with being an early riser, you cower under the covers just so you can enjoy a fleeting moment of blissful slumber.

Why do you do that? Why do you decide to push back something you know will make you more effective and successful? The answer to these questions and similar ones is a lack of *self-mastery.*

If you can habitually make yourself do that thing you dread doing, the world will be your oyster. Think about it, if after the alarm goes, instead of stretching your arm to snooze it and then covering up, you habitually **WILL** yourself to kick off those covers on day one for 100 days without fail. Do you think you would ever again struggle with snoozing your alarm?

If instead of putting off something you know you should do now to a later time or date, you simply did it and continued doing so day after day, would you ever have to battle procrastination, unsuccessfully ever again? The answer is NEVER!

How do you become a habitual self-master?

The answer to this is simple: **become proactive.** Everything in your life boils down to decisions. Dr. Myles Munroe put it very beautifully when he said, *"Our life is the sum total of all the decisions we make every day, and those decisions are determined by our priorities."*

Ultimately, we are in charge of everything in our lives. If there is one thing man has been gifted with, it would be the gift of choice. Unfortunately, because we make decisions every single moment of the day, most of us make decisions on automatic only to have to react to their repercussions much later.

Effective and successful people are proactive: they make proactive decisions and take proactive action. Unlike reactive people who adopt a wait and see stance (what we call a passive stance), proactive people do not wait to react to situations: they proactively contemplate situations and then come up with solutions.

Proactive people understand that they have responsibility or as Steven Covey puts it **response-ability.** Response-ability is the ability to decide your response to any situation or stimuli or as Mr. Covey so eloquently says, *"It is our willing permission, our consent to what happens to us, that hurts us far more than what happened to us in the first place."*

To be proactive towards behavior change (to embark on the process of self-mastery), think of what you can do; Mr. Covey calls this the **circle of influence**. The circle of influence consists of things you can change right now. For instance, instead of snoozing that morning alarm, choose to do the smallest thing of the new behavior. In the alarm example, the smallest thing would be to get yourself out of the alluring confines of the cover.

Take responsibility because ultimately, your response-ability shall determine how you react to each cue of the habit and your ability to practice the routine that follows the cue.

As you seek to develop and adopt any other habit, start with mastering the habit of self-mastery.

2: Successful People Keep Their Eyes on the Price/They Focus on the Bigger Picture

In the instance of procrastination—a bad habit that without a doubt will affect your success, you procrastinate because you fail to focus on the end goal or because the end goal is not very clear. When a vision of what you want to achieve is as clear as a cloudless blue sky, you can bet that your response-ability shall improve.

Irrespective of which habit you want to cultivate, always start with making the destination/vision/end goal as clear as day in your mind. When the image of what you want to achieve is clear, your motivation to achieve whatever you want shall be high and so shall be your ability to take immediate action once the cue presents.

For example, if the habit you want to develop is that of waking up at 5 o'clock every day, use your creative mind to create an alluring image of what doing so shall help you achieve–the end goal you have in mind. Will waking up that early give you an hour or two to work on your business plan? Will waking up early give you a chance to exercise and thus live a healthier life? Will it give your day a nice head start? Visualize the end goal as clearly as you can so you can feel motivated to exercise self-mastery.

3: Effective and Successful People Habitual Prioritize

Unfortunately, even though most of us are busy throughout the day, what we end up accomplishing is the 80% that barely influences our effectiveness or success. To be effective and successful, you have to prioritize.

While you may have a ton of tasks on your To-do list, the tasks on your To-do list are not equal. Some are more important. To be effective and successful, you have to get into the habit of prioritizing every aspect of your life and above all, choose to do that which fuels your effectiveness and success.

When you are creating new habits, you can categorize everything you need to do (to make the habit habitual) into two categories: important and urgent; this is according to the time management matrix:

	Urgent	Non-Urgent
Important	**Q-1: Quadrant of Necessity** • Impending deadlines (that are important and have long-term consequence to your life) • Crises/Emergencies • Resolving immediate problems • Certain e-mails that may change your life (e.g., job app, biz opport)	**Q-2: Quadrant of Quality and Personal Leadership** • Building long-term solutions/systems • Relationship building • Building your dream career/business • Personal/Skill development • Improving your health/wellness • Finding your life partner
Not Important	**Q-3: Quadrant of Deception** • Interruptions/Distractions • Most phone calls/e-mails • Attending inconsequential meetings • Spending a lot of time on a task (report, e-mail) that has little to no impact to your goals/life in long run • Dealing with others' requests	**Q-4: Quadrant of Waste** • Mindless TV/web surfing / chatting • Reading gossip sites/forums • Watching/reading news (to an extent) • Certain phone calls/e-mails • Excessive gaming • Idling • Any time wasting activity

Our focus should be on the second quadrant, which is the epitome of effective time management. This quadrant is all about being effective, creating effective plan of action for whatever behavior change we want to implement, and doing the things we want to do but because we lack self-mastery, we never do. Prioritizing this quadrant is what shall make you effective and successful.

On the other hand, when we concentrate on the first quadrant, we spend all our time reacting to problems and crises. Because the problems and crises constantly get bigger and bigger, we have to put out more fires, our stress increases, we put off things, and eventually, we experience burnout and give up the habits we were trying to adopt in the first place.

If we pay attention to the third quadrant, we also spend our time being reactive instead of proactive; we spend all our time reacting to things we consider urgent while in reality, their urgency is nothing if not a perceived urgency. Focusing on this quadrant leads to short-term focus.

When we focus on the fourth quadrant, we lead irresponsible lives. This is what happens when we practice a habit such as after a day at work, sitting for hours on end in front of the T.V and watching TV late into the night while we know we should wake up earlier and prepare for the day. In the end, we end up rushing through our morning and then rushing through the entire day feeling overwhelmed and trying to catch up.

4: Successful People Are Consistent

As we stated earlier, consistency is at the core of developing any habit. If you start practicing a specific habit today, quit tomorrow, practice it the day after, and then quit after, you will never make that habit stick.

To practice consistency, you have to master yourself. Refer to the discussion on how to do that.

In any case, as long as you are not consistent in what you do, you will not be develop the good habit, since the very core of habits is repeated behavior, bad or good. One great way of doing being consistent is making a habit a daily occurrence.

Do it daily

Anything you set out to do in the course of trying to develop a habit demands that you do not skip a day. When you have determine how to break a habit, you will achieve your goal by repeating the resolved process of breaking it every day, preferably at the same time each day, and the same way until it sticks and gets to a point where when you do not do it, you feel as if something is missing from your life.

Motivation

Successful people always consider the aspect of motivation as they plan how to be consistent in developing good habits or breaking bad ones. Why do you want to build a specific habit? Having weighed the pros and cons, you will immediately feel motivated to repeat the action. Think about all the benefits and positives you will gain when you do it, and the negatives or consequences that will come or linger when you do not do it. As a successful person already, think of this each time you begin losing motivation. You need to stay on track.

"Motivation is what gets you started. Habit is what keeps you going." -Jim Rohn

Reward yourself

At the start, you might not really derive any noticeable benefits from engaging in some habits (except some tinge of feel good feeling). This can make it very easy to give up if you don't have the needed 'fire' to keep going. So what do you do in that case? Well, your best bet is to 'bribe' yourself into doing whatever it is that needs to be done to build the habit. The reason why bad habits like alcohol, porn addiction, gambling and smoking are so easy to build is that they tend to give people 'instant' gratification right from the beginning. That's why many people want to try again tomorrow even if their first experience was not pleasant!

Therefore, as you build any habit, you should strive to ensure that whatever it is that you engage in gives you the much needed gratification so that you come again tomorrow looking forward for another experience. Therefore, find a reward that you can peg your habit building activities on then make sure to reward yourself whenever you engage in the desired activity.

If you can master these four habits, you shall be effective and successful. These habits encapsulate every other habit you need to develop to be affective and to achieve success.

Next, we will discuss some creative ways to make the habits you want to build to stick.

How To Make The Good Habits Stick

Secrets That Influential People Use To Stick To Their Habits

Yes, you have learned all about how to create habits and the habits of the effective and successful but what is the guarantee that you will actually stick to them? Have you asked yourself, why these influential people seem to get so much done yet when you try chasing similar goals, it's a wild goose chase?

The difference is that many people do not understand that there is a big difference between wanting to change something and actually changing it. You might adapt and create these new habits but along the way, you lose your motivation and psych due to some negative factors. This in turn discourages you and you end up frustrated with not attaining your goals.

Therefore, sticking to your newly formed habits is important in ultimately reaching the goals you aimed for when you started this process of habit transformation. Creating and sustaining these good habits does not have to be necessarily difficult if you have a good plan to prevent yourself from backsliding. That is why you need strategies to help you stick to them for good. Here are some of the strategies to help you avoid setbacks and instead make sure you stick to your newly formed habits for good:

Start Small In Your Habits And Progressively Grow

The problem with most of us is that we want to grow rich overnight and that is why instead of working from scratch and progressively growing, we want to become rich as quickly as possible. It is not bad to want more in life but make sure that you do not become greedy because patience pays.

If you quickly jump to bigger and more difficult habits, it will require you to use a significant amount of effort and will power. These two things work like a muscle, when you extend a muscle too much, it becomes tired; that is why you will be most likely to quit and go back to your old habits.

To avoid all this from happening after going through all that hustle, make sure you start doing the habits small before moving up a notch. If you want to change your diet instead of suddenly changing to the new habit quickly, start by adding vegetables to your normal diet and slowly implement other components of the diet. Before you know it, you will have achieved your goal of having your new habit slowly without rushing into it.

Remember always that you should aim on establishing the actual behavior first before moving to the more technical parts of the behavior. Do not increase the effort in behavior before it has become a natural part of you.

Make Sure That The Habit Is Implemented

Performing the habit continuously is the first step in making it autonomic. However, how can you keep doing the habit if you forget occasionally? Well, the best option is to make sure that you devise ways to help make sure you do not forget. Remember that these habits are new in your life and therefore, having to keep up with them everyday might be difficult. You need to have clear intentions and that is why poor intentions like "I will try eating a healthy diet whenever I can" will not cut it.

The first step in making sure that you implement the habits is to create an implementation intention. You have to refrain yourself from being pessimistic and disorganized when you use "I will try" to make statements concerning your habits. You have to be sure and optimistic and say "Whenever I'm eating anything, I will make sure that it is healthy and beneficial to my body."

Another good way to make sure you implement the habits is by linking your newly formed habit to an already existing one. Either, you can perform the new habit before the existing one or you can perform it after doing the already existing one. This strategy works best if you link two habits that are almost similar or can lead to the other in a way. For example, after eating a healthy breakfast, you have to eat a fruit before walking out. This way, you will always remember to eat a fruit once you take your breakfast. Make sure you try linking the habits and the first few times, try to observe if it is working out; if not, link the habit to another habit until you get it right.

Implementing scheduling is yet another good way to prevent you from forgetting to do your newly formed habits. Always remember that what gets scheduled gets done. For very important habits, give them space in your schedule so that you can avoid not having time or chance to perform them.

Prepare For Failure

Man is to error. Nobody is perfect and that is why occasionally we fail in the things we do. This does not however mean that every time you fail, its due to nature. One thing these influential people do is that they plan ahead for failure because they know everything they do is a risk and there is a probability of it failing.

Once you have formed a new habit and along the way you backslide and find yourself going back to your old habit, don't be hard on yourself. Instead of crying over spilt milk, design ways in which you will stop yourself from repeating the mistakes in the future. Better still; think of possible failures that you may get along the way and think of ways to prevent either of them from happening. This way, you will prevent the likelihood of giving up due to several failures along the way.

Surround Yourself With Beneficial People

If you are trying to change a bad habit of eating healthy foods and your friend keeps on pulling you to have a bite, you are more likely to give in to the temptation. Therefore, if you surround yourself with people who contribute a lot to your bad old habits then you are definitely going to fail in achieving your goals. You need to surround yourself with people who are only concerned with making sure that you transform and stick to your habits completely i.e. people who are there to help you when you fall down and people who are there to motivate you to keep going by helping you out.

In fact, strive to make these people your accountability partners by declaring your intentions to them (it doesn't have to be a large group of people). In so doing, you will 'feel the pressure' to impress your accountability partners, which means you will do everything in your power to ensure the habit you are striving to build sticks. If you feel that verbal commitments are not enough, you can make money part of your conversation. Give someone a certain amount of money, which you pledge to lose if you do not follow a certain set of habits or activities over a certain period. In so doing, you will be under pressure not to lose your money, which in the end will work in your favor since you will ultimately build your desired habits.

I Need Your Help...

We have come to the end of the book. Thank you for reading and congratulations for reading until the end.

I hope this book was able to help you to build good habits.

The next step is to take action.

Finally, if you enjoyed this book, then I'd like to ask you for a favor, would you be kind enough to leave a review for this book on Amazon? It'd be greatly appreciated!

I want to reach as many people as I can with this book, and more reviews will help me accomplish that!

Thank you and good luck!

Preview Of 'Freedom: How To Make Money Online And Become Financially Free By Creating Passive Income'

Before you can learn the specifics of building a passive income, it is critical that you understand what you are venturing into so that you don't start with a wrong idea of what it is you are working towards as well as what to expect from your efforts. Let's begin.

Passive Income: A Comprehensive Background

A passive income, also called a residual income, is simply the money you earn when you are not actively working. If you are actively working, it means you will receive some money (active income), which, when you stop working, you stop earning. With contract work or active work, you have to do some work to receive pay. In other words, you MUST exchange your time (hours, minutes, days, weeks or even months) for pay. In that case, if you are not working, you cannot be paid; it is simple logic!

This is always not the case with a passive income. With passive incomes, you earn whether you work actively or not. To create a passive income stream, you will have to put in some work upfront to get the ball rolling. You will however get to a point where your income stream will become passive such that it generates revenue on its own without you having to work for it. Think of publishing a book on Amazon for instance. After doing the upfront work of writing and promoting the book in its initial stages, you will get to a point whereby the book can continue making money whether you do anything to promote it or not. That's passive income!

Before we head any further, we have to discuss some things about a passive income because these things are important and will help you understand the nature of a passive income. Some of these include:

1: Passive incomes are often not permanent incomes: Get it right: some online passive incomes may last for years, decades, or even centuries. They can however never be permanent. This is because all forms of income eventually dry up at a given point for one reason or another.

2: It is not a one-time lump sum payment: Some incomes such as inheritance, sale of assets like pieces of land, or sale of stocks are one-time lump sum payments. This is not the case with passive income since a passive income is a source of income that has a sense of continuity over a certain period.

3: Some passive incomes are semi-passive: You may be your own boss but you will need to do some work (even if its management), although you will not receive pay for maintaining your investment.

For instance, if you build a house and rent it out, you will definitely receive your passive income from the tenants but when they move out, you will have to invest some energy, money, and time to maintain the vacated premise and seek other tenants.

4: Passive income streams need maintenance: Whether it is checking emails or paying taxes on your passive income, you have to do some of these activities for maintenance since they keep your source of passive income going.

5: Your passive income might be another person's active Income: No matter what kind of online business you invest in, you will have to hire people to do some work that help you earn your passive income. In other words, your passive income builds on leveraging on other people's active income to succeed! For example, if you have a freelance writing marketplace for instance, you will have to hire some people who will be writing or editing your articles. You will have to pay them hence they will receive active income but their work is what shall help you earn a passive income.

Now that we have established these critical things about passive income streams, the next thing we have to consider is why the internet is the best way to create multiple passive income streams.

Check out the rest of Freedom: How To Make Money Online And Become Financially Free By Creating Passive Income on Amazon, go to: http://amzn.to/2nTo80C

Check Out My Other Books

Below you'll find some of my other popular books that are popular on Amazon and Kindle as well. Simply click on the links below to check them out. Alternatively, you can visit my author page on Amazon to see other work done by me.

20 Easy And Fast Diet Tips For Losing Weight – An Easy-To-Follow Weight Loss Guide

Belly Diet: The Zero Belly Diet Step-By-Step Guide Which Will Help You To Lose Your Belly And Enjoy Your Flat Belly

Anti-Inflammatory Diet Guide – The Guide To Reduce Inflammation And Live A Healthy Life Without Pain

Dash Diet: Cookbook For Weight Loss With Action Plan And Easy Recipes

Clean Eating: Cookbook And Guide To Restore Your Body's Natural Balance And Eat Healthy

Negative Calorie Diet: Cookbook & Guide Which Help You To Burn Body Fat, Lose Weight And Live Healthy

Smart Fat: Cookbook With Fat Meals Which Help You To Lose Weight, Get Healthy And Improve Brain Function

Freedom: How To Make Money Online And Become Financially Free By Creating Passive Income

www.ingramcontent.com/pod-product-compliance
Lightning Source LLC
Chambersburg PA
CBHW071242220526

45468CB00002B/963